THE BOY CALLED
INCERTO

CHRISTINE MARANO

ISBN 978-1-63885-365-7 (Paperback)
ISBN 978-1-63885-366-4 (Digital)

Covenant Books, Inc.
11661 Hwy 707
Murrells Inlet, SC 29576
www.covenantbooks.com

The cozy autumn days and crisp fall nights were upon us. Golden leaves fluttered gently to the ground. The crunch of fallen leaves could be heard underfoot. It is the season to behold nature's palette ablaze with a mosaic of color: of reds, yellows, and burnt gold.

The warm embrace of an amber afternoon and the promise of a wonderful life make autumn the most romantic and heartwarming season.

And yet, this feeling of warmth and comfort seemed to have eluded me this fall day. My rather quiet felines, who enjoyed curling up and basking in the fireplace glow, became restless, pouncing from sofa to recliner, back again to sofa, landing in a pierced-like trance staring motionless out of the bowed-like window. Then they began to scratch at the shuttered blinds in a frenzy, bouncing again from sofa to chair and back again!

I looked at my husband, and he at me, perplexed and alarmed. We gently lifted the blind, turned on the porch light, and gasped in dismay.

There on the umbrella glass table rested a basket entirely cloaked with a handwoven shawl. Then through the shine of the harvest moon was illuminated a slight movement, a whimpered cry. In one swift movement, this basket was whisked from the table and brought into the welcomed warmth of home, into the arms of love.

Frantically, with trembling fingers, shaking hands, the infant was disrobed. This tiny body shuddered to the touch; it shivered. With great care and gentleness, this tiny body was placed against my breast, enveloped in my arms, breathing in the warmth and love that would follow him to his destiny.

Swaddled under my nightgown covered by my robe, head nestled under my chin, this fragile newborn was enveloped in love. The beat of his heart began in cadence with mine. The pink flesh-tone began to slowly return to his face, his hands, his quivering body, his entire being.

Quickly, my husband warmed his clothes in the dryer. He searched the basket for milk, diapers, any sustenance he could find. He did, along with a handwritten note.

> Miss Angelisa, I leave my heart and my soul to you. I cannot take care of my baby boy. I do not have anyone to watch over him except you. His father abandoned me. I have no job, and I have no security or safety. I must return to my homeland, but my son must stay! He must grow up, become a man, and love this country.
>
> I love you, Miss Angelisa, as I love my son. Share each other's love.
>
> My heart cries…my soul weeps.

John and Carl, Angelisa's sons, twelve and eight years old respectively, came from upstairs, running to see what the commotion was.

Just then, the wailing of sirens could be heard off in the distance, a cornucopia of bright lights flashing like autumn leaves falling to the ground. The incessant pounding at the door, drumming along with my beating heart, startled me.

Two young paramedics rushed in followed by two older police officers shrouded in a cloud of blue. The young medic leaned forward to take the baby from my arms; this infant melded to my breast! I flinched, wrestled away from their clutches, and drew this child, this child who would become an extension of my being, even closer to my body. Then the officers entered, calmly saying, "Miss, we are here to take this baby to the hospital to check him over, to see that he hasn't been harmed or if he's in need of medical attention, ASAP."

Struggling again, I managed to shout, "Please, you must take me with him! I will not let him go! Please, there is a piercing chill in the air. He needs to feel the warmth of my body, the beating of my heart. I will ride along until inside the hospital. To the doctor only, will I release this innocent, this extension of myself."

The medics then brought in a portable service chair, gently seating and strapping us in securely. As they carried us to the waiting ambulance, the fall mist encircled us, the flashing lights illuminated us, and the smell of the burning wood of a fireplace comforted us.

John and Carl were told to stay at home and wait for their aunt Jen until we returned from the hospital.

*****

Upon entering the emergency room at the children's hospital, a bevy of nurses, attendants, and personnel swarmed around pushing, pulling, eager to attend to this foundling, this waif who was given up by his mother, by her love for him to be entrusted to another's love.

After being brought into the examining room, still clutching to this innocent, she was approached by a young thirtyish-looking doctor.

"Mrs. Altomonte, you must release this child to me for examination."

"You will bring him back to me?" she asked, looking intensely at him.

"In due time," he mumbled, and off they went through the wide swinging doors down the long corridor, disappearing out of sight.

Fear enveloped her, wrapping its tentacles around her entire being, strangling her breath, and stealing her heart's beat. Just then, her husband found her shivering and weeping. He gently enfolded her in his arms, whispering words of comfort and encouragement.

"Don't worry, he's a strong little guy. He will be just fine. You'll see."

Still shivering, Angelisa turned to her husband, with such fear in her eyes and cried out, "He is not coming back to us, to me. They will take him away from us!"

"Who? He was left in our care, on our deck, at our house! Who? Were you told this…who said this…why do you think this?"

She could sense it like a shroud covering her…she felt lifeless, limp. She screamed inside, but no cries came out of her. She was so scared.

Moments later, the young doctor approached, walking quietly yet gingerly, his clean crisp white coat rustling against his pants.

"The child is fine. Obviously, well cared for. I assume his age to be about seven weeks. He is sleeping comfortably. However, hospital policy is that we keep the child for observation to be sure everything is functioning well."

"When can I see him? Visit him? Hold him?"

"That I cannot answer. But a representative from Social Services will be meeting with you soon."

"Social Services, why? When?"

"All your questions will be addressed then. Nice meeting you, and good luck."

*****

Moments later, in the distance, walking toward Angelisa and her husband was Ms. Allen. With an extended hand, Ms. Allen greeted them.

"How nice to meet you both. My name is Ms. Allen, social worker from the Department of Children and Families. I have been assigned to investigate this case regarding the abandonment of this child, Baby Doe."

Baby Doe…Baby Doe! The words spun around in my head like a swirling vortex.

"Why, why, Ms. Allen, do you refer to this child as Baby Doe? He is not an object! He is an infant, a boy child…a baby boy…not a nameless Baby Doe!"

"Tomorrow, we will address this situation, Mrs. Altomonte. Until then, goodbye."

Reluctantly, tears in my eyes and a dagger through my heart, we left the hospital, leaving the life that was entrusted to me be swaddled in unknown arms, be placed in an unknown bassinet with no one to hold him, to rock him, to sing to him. No one to share the beating of his heart.

Finally, I closed my eyes and cried myself to sleep. Tomorrow was a new day and a new battle ahead…one I was determined not to lose.

*****

And so, the new dawn arose with hues of lavender, pink, and rose. Such glory in the universe, such sorrow in my soul. Was my Gift from God to be taken from me as swiftly as it had been given?

But this new morning, this new day, I must share with my sons, must quell their fears, must answer all questions.

But I had work to do: meet with Ms. Allen, the social worker, visit baby with no name. My baby has a name…a given name, *Incerto*.

We had agreed to meet at the hospital. I prayed to see Incerto and maybe even hold him in my arms. But that was not to be. When I arrived, there was Ms. Allen sitting quite erect, professional looking, with matching woolen gloves, hat, and scarf of blended, muted shades of brown, yellow, and burgundy reflective of the season ready to usher in, winter.

She turned to signal me to meet her. Holding assured and polite, I greeted her as I thought to myself, *Ms. Allen I am glad to meet with you so we can address this situation so we can get the wheels of bureaucracy moving so I can hold that given child left on my deck, left in my care, left in my arms, enfolded in my love.*

"First, Mrs. Altomonte, let me go over the process and steps that are put in place when a child is abandoned…"

"Excuse me, Ms. Allen, the child wasn't abandoned. He was placed intentionally by his birth mother in my care. Not abandoned. And the child is not Baby Boy Doe. He is a person with identity. I call him Incerto."

"All well and good, Mrs. Altomonte, but procedure must be followed. And it has been up to this point. You rescued the child, called the police, brought him to the hospital, and now the Department of Children and Families, DCF, will have custody of this child until a determination is made as to placement, foster care, and ultimately adoption."

"*Placement! Foster care! Adoption!* What are you saying! He belongs in my care!"

"In order for that to happen, Mrs. Altomonte, you must go through the process. You must fill out the necessary forms to ultimately have the child placed in your care as a foster parent. You must first petition the court for foster care, followed by an interview. A background check will have to be conducted as well. This, Mrs. Altomonte, takes time, sometimes weeks, months, and even longer. Prepare yourself for this process. Seek out professional guidance. Start this procedure immediately. There are always good, decent young couples waiting for the opportunity to become foster parents, especially of an infant."

And with that, Angelisa trudged slowly toward her home, no longer feeling the warmth of a glowing fire and the smell of chestnuts or pumpkins or the sound of rustling leaves. And yet with all this beauty, Angelisa knows there is a certain foreshadowing of a long cold winter. She ponders the fact that in everyone's lifetime, some heartache may come, but she feels in God's love she will endure.

And so the following day, Angelisa placed two calls that will change her destiny forever, one to the Department of Children and Families, DCF, and the other to Philip Cohen, attorney. He will become her legal guide, her hope, her voice, Incerto's voice.

*****

With fear and trepidation, Angelisa entered the judge's chamber. Her eyes widened, scanning the old-fashioned décor of the room. Mahogany-veneered walls lined with over stacked bookshelves; national and state flags adorned the opposite wall. On the side wall prominently placed is a framed photograph of the current president.

The room itself was sparsely furnished. The conference table of mahogany veneer with claw ball feet was placed at the rear of the room. Around the table were several sturdy dark-brown leather-padded high back chairs.

A tense, unsettling quiet permeated the air. The deadening silence was broken when Judge Obrien, a robust rose-cheeked gentleman of fifty, entered the chamber, inviting all to be seated. He had a rather calm yet serious countenance about him. This was encouraging and helped Angelisa to relax momentarily. After a few seconds of perusing the file and documents before him and clearing his throat, he called out the names of the parties before him.

Then the proceedings began; her heart pounded rapidly in her chest, hands trembling, throat dry, lips parched, and quiet deep breaths.

And then it all began.

The first person to respond to the judge's questions was Attorney Cohen, presenting the circumstances of the case while supporting our belief that we would be the best caregivers, foster parents, and ultimately family for the child.

Judge Obrien then called on Ms. Allen, who stood facing the judge, gave an overview of my interview, my encounter, and yes, my forceful questioning of the judicial system. She then placed the report on his desk, made no eye contact but turned and scurried out of the chamber.

Next, Mr. Cohen, with the judge's consent, presented documents supporting my moral character both professionally and personally from colleagues, family, friends, and students.

One young special-needs student wrote for morning work five reasons to the question why Miss Angelisa is a good teacher.

He lists five reasons why Mrs. Angelisa is the best.

> Number 1 sheh's very Kind.
> Number 2 sheh's funny.
> Number 3 sheh's carring.
> Number 4 sheh's generous.
> Last but not least, she dose not use volgaradys.
> She makes me happy when I see her.

This and many other documents were presented along with recommendations not only from colleagues but also from school administrators, parents, and students with the goal for Judge Obrien to look positively and favorably on his client.

And then, he turned to me to give my reasons, my defense, my support for myself as to why I am the best qualified person to be mother, guardian, defender, and protector of this child, this sweet, innocent, abandoned by love but placed in the care of my love.

"Thank you, your honor. I come before you to present my plea to find in my favor of giving back to me this fragile but loved child who was taken from my arms to go to another's. His mother did not just 'abandon' him. She did not leave him on the street, or in a trash can. No! She entrusted him to me, she left him for me! She did not drop him through a shoot or leave him on police steps or at any of the safe havens! She left him in my care! As you read her note, please pause where she writes, 'But my son must stay! He must grow up, become a man, and love this country.' And she closes with 'I love you, Miss Angelisa, as I love my son. Share each other's love.'"

Gathering my composure, I stated calmly, "Your honor, I would ask the court's permission to visit the infant in the hospital nursery. As we know, your honor, the first three months, in fact, the first three years of an infant's life, is most crucial for emotional attachments as well as language development. And that is what I wish for this precious human being. Thank you, your honor, for hearing my plea."

With that, we left the courthouse.

*****

That evening, as I decided to take a quick walk, I could feel the wind pushing against me, smell a pile of raked leaves, and see pumpkins sitting aglow on neighbors' doorsteps.

And yet, I felt with all the beauty of fall comes a certain sadness of the changing colors, foreshadowing the coming of a long, cold winter. Could this be a foreshadowing of what is to come for me and for Incerto?

The following morning with a crisp freshness in the air, a kaleidoscope of leaves falling to the ground, and the swishing of leaves beneath my shoes, I felt rejuvenated that with a new season approaching, requiring strength and fortitude to endure those sun-filled days and long harsh cold New England nights, there would be a new beginning to follow.

So with a jaunt in my step, I entered the children's hospital, excitement in my heart for I was going to see Incerto, and not Baby Boy Doe. I brought with me a medal of the Blessed Mother Mary's mother, St. Ann, Guardian of Babies, to pin to Incerto's bassinet to be watched over, to let no harm come to him, the very medal that was found among his belongings when disrobed that evening at my home.

After obtaining permission by the head nurse to visit, I gingerly stepped into the nursery. A nurse approached me and asked for the child's name. My reply was to inform her the baby had not yet been given a name until this moment. I then slipped into the name tag his name, Incerto. Smiling, she showed me the way to *my* baby. The most precious sight in all the world, the most precious gift anyone would receive, the most proof that, yes, there is a God in heaven and on earth.

Tears welling up in my eyes, I carefully pinned the medal of St. Ann to the side of his bassinet. With hands trembling, heart pounding, and stomach churning, I slowly lifted up into my arms this gift of love, Incerto.

Sitting in the rocker, I inhaled the sweet smell of his body, a baby's scent. I smothered his entire being with loving kisses from head to toes, from eyes to ears, from curled fist to curled toes. And then I just embraced him in my arms, sat rocking and humming sweet melodies as I drifted into an ethereal haze.

With every step taken, Angelisa would visit the nursery daily, greeting the nursery monitor. Once inside she would hold, rock, sing, and smother with the kind of love that only a mother could give to her child, Incerto. After placing the child down for a nap, she would walk through the nursery, straighten other crib blankets, hold, hum, rock, and sing to the other *babies with no names.*

This became a part of Angelisa's daily routine, walking through the rustle of dry leaves, listening to the squeals of joy as children walked to school, breathing in the smell of freshly raked leaves, watching football playing in the distance. Fall was surely upon us.

*****

The following morning, having served breakfast to her family hurriedly, Angelisa was asked by her elder son, John, where she was going in such a rush.

"To the hospital, John. You know that."

"Why, every morning, we don't talk or even see you that much anymore."

"Yeah, Mom," piped up Carl. "I miss you. Don't you miss us anymore?"

Angelisa stood frozen in her step. Truth be told, she did not realize the effect her all-consuming attention on Incerto had on her sons, her babies. She knew she had to answer to her sons, even to her husband.

Tonight, I will do this. I must. I cannot lose them. I love them too much. I am them, and they are me.

*****

That evening after dinner, as a family, we gathered in the family room with the inviting glow and comforting smell of the wood burning in the fireplace as John snuggled against me, and Carl cuddled with his Dad.

"John and Carl, my dear sons, I heard what you were saying to me this morning. Now you both know that we always share whatever it is that needs sharing. This is one of those times. Your father and I understand your feelings of being ignored or not listened to especially since this baby boy was left to us to care for and to love. I know it is difficult to understand this all at once. But be assured, we love you and always will. This baby is all alone. All alone tonight in a place he senses is not his own. He does not feel the warmth of his mother's arms or the kisses on his cheeks. Do you understand what I am saying?"

"I think I do," in an almost inaudible voice, whispered John.

"ME TOO!" shouted Carl!

"John, do you remember when you were little and saw the shadows on the walls? What did you do then?"

"I remember being afraid and running to your bedroom."

"And what did you do next?"

"I jumped on the bed, and you and Dad snuggled me between you and talked to me and settled me down."

"And you, Carl? Do you remember when you were a tiny little boy?"

"I used to have nightmares. Monsters were chasing me. I was really scared and cried a lot!"

"And then what happened?"

"You would come to my room, talk to me about monsters and dinosaurs."

"And when you calmed down, and I thought you were asleep, and I returned to my bedroom, I would hear little footsteps behind me and feel someone climb into the bed with me and Dad. Do you remember? Do you both remember the warm, safe, happy feeling you felt? I know you do. Now think of our little special baby who was left to us as a gift from God. That is how your Dad and I felt about you, a gift from God. Think. When this baby boy cries or is frightened, is there someone there to hold him, cuddle him in bed? We know there is not. So, John and Carl, do you not think you can share some, just a little bit, of the love you already have with this baby boy?"

"You're right, Mom. I guess there's plenty enough love here to share with that little baby."

"Mom, what are we to call him? Baby?"

"Well, I think I have picked a name for this baby boy that all of us will understand. INCERTO!"

"That's a different name. It's not American like ours."

Well, Carl, you are right. It is not. It is a name that may be Latino or Hispanic or even Italian. Baby Incerto's mother is not from here, America, but from another country. I want Incerto to always be reminded of his birth culture and the heritage of his birth mother. Do you understand?"

"Yes," they replied in unison.

"Let's play a game, okay? Try to guess Baby Incerto's name in English! *In* as in 'invisible,' what would that mean?"

"Not visible, can't see you," piped up Carl.

"So, what does *in* mean, boys?"

"Not!" they shouted.

"Now let's figure out "cert-o." Say you know the answer to a question, you raise your hand to answer because you are? Tell me, John."

Pausing for a moment, he shouts out, "Sure! You are sure, certain of your answer."

"Great! Now let's put both English words together."

In unison, they shouted, "Not sure! Incerto means not sure!"

"I know why, Mom. No one is sure or knows who his mom is. Am I right?"

"You guys are soooo smart! But you know he has a second name, a middle name, *Giancarlo.*

So, let's see who can figure out how your Dad and I came up with this name, okay? Think about it. Just look at the whole name and see if you can find one real name."

"Carl, my name. It's in Carlo but no *o!*"

"Great! How about Gian?" Long pause. "Well, maybe saying it really fast you may hear a name you recognize. Let's try it!"

And so, they all tried saying Gian as loudly and quickly creating a cacophony of sound.

"I have it!" shouted John. "It's my name, John!"

"So now, what are the names of my three boys?"

In unison they all shouted, "John, Carl, and Incerto!"

Proud with themselves, John and Carl hugged one another and went to sleep, *each in his own bed.*

Now, this gift from God has a real name, Incerto Giancarlo.

With that said, Angelisa closed her eyes, nestling safely in the warm embrace of her husband.

*****

Angelisa entered the hospital daily, settling into this almost mesmerizing routine. She became quite friendly with the head nurse, Ellen Quinn, who greeted her with a smile and a warm hug each morning. Now it was Angelisa who greeted Nurse Quinn with a hot pumpkin drink and a muffin.

That morning, Nurse Quinn called her aside. "Angelisa, I noticed you added a name to the baby card, *Incerto*. What is that all about?"

Angelisa moved closer to nurse Quinn and in a quiet hushed voice said, "It's my great-grandfather's name… It means of unknown parentage. You see, he, too, was a foundling." And so Angelisa shared the family story of how her great-grandfather came to be known as Virgilio Incerto.

The history of my great-grandfather was researched and considered to be true. His mother, whose name was never known, or if it were, was never revealed, was from a poor village in Italy. And being poor, as were most peasants in those days, she sought work to help her family. As it turned out, this beautiful sixteen-year-old young girl went to work in the Palatso Reale for the Duke of Savoy. It was asserted that the duke was later known as King Victor Emmanuel II. Needless to say, this young maid's beauty attracted the attention of the master of the house. The story told of this sweet young thing becoming the "plaything" of the master.

She became romantically involved with the duke. She conceived and gave birth to a blonde blue-eyed boy.

Covered with a richly decorated blanket, he was placed in an intricately woven basket and left at the door of the convent where the good sisters would find him. This young mother could have, however, dropped him down a chute where others would find and care for him. This was a much common practice in Europe at the time. Much like our safe haven system. But this infant's mother wanted him cared for by the good nuns and the household of the duke. At the time he was dropped off, the Feast of St. Virgilio was being celebrated; therefore, the child was named Virgilio, and since neither parent was *unknown*, his name became Incerto, the meaning of which is unknown parentage.

It is unknown what became of Virgilio's mother. It was rumored that she could have been paid off to keep her quiet or forcibly moved to another country or even killed to keep the truth from becoming known. The fact is she was never heard from again. Virgilio, however, fared far better than she. Although raised by the nuns, he spent a good deal of time in the home of the duke. At the age of fourteen, he went to live there permanently.

He became a Vatican Swiss Guard. By that age, he was about six feet tall and stood very erect. This posture he carried with him all his life. When reaching the age of seventeen, he became an expert horseman. He was then placed in the cavalry, a very prestigious appointment.

*****

My great-grandfather married, had six children, then journeyed to America, living a most comfortable life. As was rumored, he took a good deal of money with him. However, his children were sworn to secrecy about his origins, thus preventing further information about his life.

Nurse Quinn looked at me with a stunned yet an amazed gaze. Quietly she said, "So now I know the reason for your all-consuming attention to this baby whose beginnings so mirror that of your great-grandfather. Interesting and fascinating. But I am afraid this is not the Italy of a small village where custom, tradition, and unbroken ties prevailed. I'm sure you know and have been told the process of placement that any abandoned child goes through with DCF to insure the best possible outcome for any child, even Incerto."

Looking at Nurse Quinn, I nodded and then in a soft, gentle, but firm voice stated that I was now the caregiver, the protector, the surrogate of Baby Incerto.

*****

By the third week of visiting the nursery, there had been no decision from the court. Angelisa put this aside and tried focusing on visiting Incerto and the other abandoned sweet innocents. As she approached the nursery, ready to greet Nurse Quinn, Dunkin' and muffin in hand, she realized that no one was there. She looked around and then placed the coffee and muffin on the desk.

She approached the nursery but felt that something was wrong, out of place. When she entered the nursery, she noticed the bassinets had been rearranged. *That's odd*, she thought. *But why?* As she walked around heading toward Incerto's area, fear gripped her. His bassinet was gone. *Did they move it to another section?* she asked. *Why wasn't I told!* A myriad of scenes and situations plagued her mind. *Where is he?* she asked running around in the nursery. Again, she asked, *Where is he?* Still darting in and out of the rows of bassinets, she began to scream, "WHERE IS HE!"

Just then, Nurse Quinn was walking toward her desk when she heard all the commotion. Quickly, she ran to Angelisa, placing her arm around her shoulder, trying to calm her but to no avail. Nurse Quinn brought her to the nurses' station, sat her down, and offered her some coffee. Refusing vehemently, Angelisa screamed, "WHERE IS HE, PLEASE TELL ME!"

Calmly, Nurse Quinn began to explain. "Angelisa, please believe me that I found out this morning when I came on duty that some necessary arrangements were made last night. When infants reached three months or older, rules were in place stating they were to be moved to another DCF-approved facility. Had I known, I would have prepared you for this moment. I did not know, believe me."

"Tell me then"—Angelisa sobbed—"what facility, and how do I get there? Tell me," she demanded.

Nurse Quinn looked away. "I am not allowed to tell you that," she whispered.

"Why! He was left in my care! I won't allow this!" screamed Angelisa.

"Be quiet, please. I will try to find out for you. Do not say another word. Rest awhile and then go, please, quietly."

And with that, head spinning, heart pounding, tears flowing, Angelisa left.

As she stepped out into the dank chilly air, cloud cover above, tremors engulfed her entire being. With dizzying footsteps, she somehow found the strength to make it home.

"Mom, what's wrong?" her family shouted.

Quivering, trembling, and sobbing, Angelisa blurted out the mystery of Incerto's disappearance.

That evening, in solitude and darkness, deep sighs and heavy breath, Angelisa shouted to the darkness, "I won't let them take my baby, I won't. He was left in my care, by the woman who loves him as much as I do. I will never stop looking for him. NEVER!"

She remembered what she was told many times that *in every person's lifetime, some heartache may occur, but in quiet solitude, God helps us to endure.* She held onto that thought.

*****

Morning arrived, a fall morning, with wilting, over-grown gardens, wind howling through the trees, and leaf-strewn paths. "But where was Incerto?" she sobbed.

As Angelisa mulled over and over her plan to locate the facility that Incerto was sent to, she heard the chimes on the deck clashing, clanging wildly in the wind. Realizing she had to bring them indoors before any damage was done, with jacket covering her head, she ran onto the porch, grabbed the chimes, turned to go back in, when her eye caught a small shiny metal box sitting on the table. She stopped, looked surprised, ran to the table, whipped up the box, and ran into the house. She placed the chimes in a basket and set the metal box on the table. Puzzled, Angelisa slowly began to open the box. The inside was covered with a soft blue velvet lining often used in a jewelry box. As Angelisa looked in, she saw a white slip of paper on which was written "Parkway Center for Infants and Toddlers, 7145 Parkway, Revere." As the note dropped from her quivering hands, thoughts swirling about in her head, she managed to sit, holding onto the table for support.

Still using the table as support, she stood up, head still swirling, walked into the family room, walked over to her husband, paused…then handed him the note…and waited.

"Angelisa, where did you get this, what does it mean?"

"Someone knows where Incerto is and is secretly giving me the information to find him. I'll find this place, and then, the rest is up to me."

That evening, as Angelisa lay in bed, wind still howling, shutters slamming against the vinyl siding, she could hear the happy chatter of trick-or-treaters below her window. She wondered if Incerto were with her, what costume would she make for him…witch, cat, pumpkin, or a baseball player like *Giancarlo Stanton*.

Yet she asked herself over and over who placed the note and the St. Ann's medal in the box. Who? It could be any one of the nurses, or the aides, or the volunteers who somehow realized what was going to happen and just couldn't let him disappear, realizing *that cruelty knows no bounds.*

*****

And so began the search for this baby who was left in her care, in her heart, in her life. *What to do?* she asked herself over and over.

Well, first things first. I will go to the Parkway Center for Infants and Toddlers, seeking to work there using some pretext, perhaps looking to work as a volunteer or an aide, anything to get inside the center. Setting the GPS to 7145 Parkway, Revere, Angelisa zoomed off to find the home.

Afternoon shadows began to form as she drove slowly up the driveway of 7145 Parkway. The driveway was rocky and bumpy; the building standing off in the distance outlined by the setting sun appeared lifeless. There weren't any Halloween decorations or lights or sounds.

She parked the car and slowly, steadily walked to the front door, and rang the bell. Expecting to hear cheery chimes ringing, she was met with a cacophony of bells, such that she jumped back from the door. Just then, a light came on and the door opened slowly.

"Hello, is this Parkway Infants and Toddlers Center?"

A petite twentyish woman appeared, answering yes in Russian. She then invited Angelisa inside.

"I hope I'm not bothering you at this time. I put your address in my GPS but still managed to get offtrack."

"What you want?" asked the doorkeeper in a whisper.

"I would like to speak to the director. I would like to work here as a volunteer. I love children, and a friend thought you might need some help taking care of the children. So, I would like to speak with the person in charge.

"I go get her, your name, please?"

"Angelisa Altomonte. Excuse me, miss, and what is your name?"

"Mila, Mila Bonivich."

As she waited in the foyer, she could see the building was an old school converted into a nursery and daycare facility. It was a two-story building with worn-out wooden floors and barren walls of beige paint. There was no life either outside the building or inside. Perhaps the actual nursery rooms were more inviting. So, she began walking the corridor, peeking between the slats on the windows to catch a peek inside. No success. Just then, the young woman came walking toward her and introduced the director, Ms. Verinka.

"This is stranger who was at the door. Her name is Angelisa."

"How you do?" she asked while extending her hand out to Angelisa. "I have been the director here five years. So, you want a job here, yes? Volunteer? What experience with children, babies, infants?" she asked in a very heavy Russian accent.

Yes. I was a teacher for children of all ages. I have a lot of experience. I pride myself on being punctual and patient. I love children, all children. I would like to help. Would you need my help? Are there many children here?"

"Twelve babies, three months to eighteen months," answered Verinka.

"Oh, I see. You must be very busy with so many babies. And the caregivers must also be very busy."

"Da, very busy."

"Well, Verinka, do you mind me calling you Verinka?"

"Nyet, in fact my name is three parts Verinka Galina Andronikova."

"Russian, I assume? Interesting and somewhat musical. Would you have time to show me around the nursery and toddler rooms tomorrow, that is if you are interested?"

"Da, come tomorrow."

Angelisa stepped out into the chilly fall air, jumped into her car, and headed home.

*****

"How did it go, Angelisa? Do they need you there?" asked her husband?

"Yeah, Mom, tell us."

Angelisa, although weary and depressed, tried to put on a "good face" for her family. Excusing herself for being tired, she headed for the stairway to the bedroom. Panic and horror began to fill her head, thinking about the babies imprisoned at the center.

You were born to dance to the beat of your own heart, she kept repeating over and over.

*****

The following morning, Angelisa prepared breakfast, assuring her children she would be home in time for supper. She ran hurriedly into the cold fall air hinting of snow on the way.

As she drove up the gravel driveway, the Parkway Center loomed ahead of her like some monstrous Greek god rising from the sea. Arriving at the front entrance, she pressed the doorbell. Seconds later, Mila appeared, greeting her pleasantly and politely. Again, she was escorted into the foyer and offered a place to hang her jacket.

The foyer walls were bare of children's pictures, cartoons, and fairy-tale characters. Just then, Director Verinka appeared at the doorway and, with an extended hand, greeted and welcomed her to the center.

"Miss Angelisa, welcome to Parkway Infant and Toddler Center. Mila will give tour, tell you duties. You will work with infants three months to six months old. Other old toddlers in another room." With a slight bow of her head, Verinka disappeared into the unlit corridor.

Mila began the tour first pointing out the obvious: the director's office, nurses' area, and bathroom. Before moving on, Angelisa asked about Nurse Kusch's schedule, after seeing her name on the desk. She knew this was crucial information for the health and safety of the babies. Mila stared at Angelisa and said that Nurse Kusch comes one time each month to check over the babies. Disguising her shock, she then asked how an emergency that may occur during the day or night be handled.

"We have not a lot emergency. Come, we continue."

Then Angelisa was led into a very large storage area, one of the converted classrooms. It appeared to be overstocked with diapers, crib sheets, baby powder, undershirts—a myriad of items necessary for infants and toddlers. Glaringly missing were soft plushy toys to cuddle, colorful pacifiers to self soothe, and snuggly blankets to be wrapped in for warmth and security…nothing for the comfort of the infants, not even a musical toy in sight.

Regaining her composure, Angelisa asked if requisition slips had to be filled out to get the necessary materials.

"Nyet," Mila replied.

Strange, I wonder how they keep track of the materials that need to be ordered. Hmm, not very businesslike, mused Angelisa.

Then it was on to the infant's nursery, the very moment Angelisa had been praying for, waiting for. Chills, sweaty palms, and quiet deep breaths, she followed Mila down the dingy hall to the last classroom on the left. Angelisa could hear soft murmurs, cries, and whispers. Suddenly the door opened and standing there were two young girls about eighteen years of age, waiting to be relieved of their duty. Mila made a rather dismissive introduction then quickly ushered Angelisa into the nursery area. An acrid odor permeated the air along with a stench of soiled wet diapers and vomit. Mila noticed the sudden shocked expression on Angelisa's face.

She avoided having to explain the situation by placing blame on the lazy, unreliable, incredibly young girls who had just left. Angelisa smiled, tight lipped, holding back her own vomit. Sweeping her eyes across the room, she counted four windows with room-darkening shades, two hanging globe ceiling lights, beige-painted walls, and old scuffed floors. A room void of all color, all life.

"Come," Mila said. "I show you around and show you the babies."

With forced smile and feigned interest, she followed Mila.

Cribs were placed in three rows of four. The sides of the crib were made of metal tubes that served as bars, two-inch thick padding served as a mattress, a delivery blanket as a covering but no bumper pads for protection. Angelisa, wordless, expressionless, continued to follow Mila, to meet the babies, to meet Incerto.

Walking through the rows of cribs, Angelisa looked closely at each baby, searching for her own precious innocent.

Finally, there in the far corner crib lay a baby, a baby with a medal pinned to his undershirt. Angelisa's heart pounded so fiercely, she felt it might burst from her chest. The temptation was so great to sweep him up in her arms, race to the door, jump in the car, and race off never to be seen again. Just then, she felt Mila's hand on her arm, questioning if she were okay. With a sudden shock, Angelisa turned to assure her that she was okay. Mila continued the tour, but all became a blur, a slur of words. How could she hear, see anything, knowing she found Incerto.

Incerto was really there. She found him! Regaining composure, Angelisa began to interact again with Mila: did the infants have names; how long was each one there; were there certain ways they liked to be held; what were their likes, dislikes. She wanted to know everything about them. This barrage of questions only added to Mila's annoyance.

"Take time, Miss Angelisa. You will care good, particularly good for foundlings, orphans, throwaway babies."

Realizing what she said, she quickly covered herself, saying, "Nyet, not me I say."

It was time to leave, to leave without a touch, a caress, a kiss.

Angelisa, being gracious, polite, and thankful, shook Mila's hand, assuring her that she would be back in the morning to begin her work.

Once in her car, heading down the gravel road, Angelisa let out the most painful, mournful cry that could possibly come from any human soul.

*****

That evening, Angelisa realized that Parkway Infant and Toddler Center was wrong, all wrong. It was like a house of sorrows: no light, no sun, no cooing, no humming, no squeals of delight. Nothing! Why? Why so void of love, happiness, life? She knew that something, someone had to do something…she had to do something! She kept repeating to herself, over and over, *You were born to dance to the beat of your own heart. This I promise.*

First, she would start by keeping a daily journal of the happenings at the center not only to have data of her own but also to use when she informs the DCF the (Children's Advocacy Group) and other organizations that oversee the operations at the center. However, this will take time. But will it be time enough to protect these babies, to keep *Incerto* safe until she can take him and keep him and love him? Nothing will stop her now. Nothing!

Angelisa's first day was full of excitement, joy, and fearful anticipation. She arrived on time, presenting a personable and polite appearance.

Upon entering, Mila greeted her and said she needed to go over a few things. Angelisa smiled and followed her into the kitchen area. After pouring coffee, selecting a donut, and sitting down, Mila placed a paper on the table in front of her. A quick glance looked like a time schedule with some minor instructions and directions. Mila then explained that this was the daily schedule and assignment for the three caretakers each assigned four babies. Mila stated that the choice of babies was no problem for her. They were to decide among themselves.

The schedule was as follows:

> 8:00–9:00 bottle feeding, 15 minutes per infant
> 9:10–9:30 diaper changing, 5 minutes per infant
> 9:30–1:30 nap time
> 1:30–2:30 bottle feeding, 15 minutes per infant
> 2:40–3:00 diaper changing, 5 minutes per infant.
> 3:00–5:00 nap time
> No cell phones or pictures allowed. No visitors.

Angelisa was given the first choice. Although glancing over at the baby Incerto, she walked over to all four babies as if inspecting them, knowing Incerto would certainly be one of them.

As time went by, Angelisa became more acclimated to the conditions but never used to them, becoming more and more determined to right them, to give new life to these innocents.

*****

Later that evening, dinner being served, John and Carl asleep, Angelisa settled in front of the comfy blazing fireplace, swaddled in her robe, notebook in hand. While curled up on the sofa, she began to record the day's activity. She rewound in her mind all that she encountered during the tour—dark and disturbingly quiet. No music, no laughs, not even the sound of cries. She noted the horrible, putrid, acidic odor that greeted her, an odor of soiled wet diapers. There were no Disney characters hung on the walls, no musical toys hanging above each crib, nor any plush toys for comfort and love.

Silence…deafening silence.

She knew she had to be compliant until she had the information and proof to shut down this house of horrors. Then she realized to her horror that the center was a replica of the old-style Russian and Ukrainian orphanages that she read about so long ago. *Could this be?* she asked herself. What else was going on; why such a huge storage area for diapers, milk, salves, blankets, yet nothing of happy plush animals or musical toys or even a pacifier to calm and soothe? Why no cell phones or pictures? Why such a strict daily schedule…why? She knew she had to get evidence to shut down the Parkway Center and put it out of existence.

Who could she confide in? Trust? How does she protect these innocents doomed to a life of mental health problems, of being deprived of all human touch, of soft embraces, the feeling of a heartbeat telling them yes, you are alive…*do you hear me, Mila, Verinka!*

*****

During the several weeks that followed, Angelisa created a world of their own for these "abandoned" babies. She began to place two infants together in the crib to feed them, cleanse, hum old songs, and rock them together. She would place them side by side during nap time, hands and feet touching. She would sing to them as she changed their diapers and soothed their irritated soft, thin skin. And kiss them. Yes, kiss them. Lots of kissing, feeling human warmth, tenderness, and love. But when will this become life for them, their own life? *Dear God, help me…let me find the way.* Again, Angelisa repeated over again, *In every person's lifetime, some heartache may occur, but in quiet solitude, God helps us endure…* How much more endurance before it was too late?

That evening while wrestling with unanswerable questions, it occurred to her that the one person who would understand, who could be trusted was Nurse Quinn—the nurse with the laughing Irish eyes and a hearty laugh to go with it, the nurse to whom she brought Dunkin' and muffins every morning, the nurse who befriended her, the nurse whom she knew intuitively had placed the silver metal box with the note inside it on her table, Nurse Quinn! *But I must get in touch with her tomorrow. I'll text her a quick note asking to meet her with some news of grave importance. Yes, that is what I'll do!*

She rested her head on the pillow, closed her eyes, and thought happy thoughts, yet determined, determined to save Incerto and the children.

The following morning, Angelisa texted Nurse Quinn, pleading to meet with her at her favorite place, Dunkin's.

*****

The chill in the air, the smell, the feel of winter around the corner gave way to a biting wind to greet Angelisa bundled in a warm parka. She entered the shop, immediately walked to the back corner, spotting Nurse Quinn also huddled against the wall seeking some warmth. Both embraced each other warmly, staring into each other's eyes while tears fell softly. Having ordered their coffee and muffin, Angelisa began to speak.

"I have followed my plan to be with Incerto at the Parkway Infant and Toddler Center. I have volunteered my services to watch over and protect him. Although I don't know who left me the note or in whose gratitude I am, I will forever be grateful until the day I have my baby back or until the day I die."

Nurse Quinn just stared at Angelisa without a blink; seconds passed, and then she spoke. "Tell me, Angelisa, what is happening? What is going on? I could read panic in your text."

And so Angelisa proceeded to share with the one person she could trust, the whole, ugly, frightful story of the happenings at the center.

Shock, dismay, and disbelief swept across Nurse Quinn's face. Angelisa could see visible tremors engulfing her entire being.

"We must do something about this and quick," insisted Nurse Quinn. "Give me time to get my wits together and plan out what our next steps will be."

The angels of hope embraced and walked their separate ways.

*****

Angelisa hopped in her car and headed toward the center, not knowing what to encounter next. As she drove up the dirt road, she could sense something was wrong. She could faintly make out the flashing of blue and red lights. As she approached the building, her heart sank, her hands shook, her lips quivered. What was an ambulance, police cars, and a crowd of people doing outside the center? Was there a fire, a baby in distress? What? Stumbling, she raced to the entrance. Mila was standing there...what was it...what happened? Mila reached to grab Angelisa and brought her in doors.

"Angelisa, horrible, happened! Two babies missing."

"Who, which ones?" screeched Angelisa. "Tell me!" she screamed, shaking Mila.

"Boy Prince and Girl Princess."

With that, Angelisa collapsed to the floor, holding her head and screaming, and crying…

"*Tell me! Tell me!*"

The EMTs ran in to assist and try to calm Angelisa, but the screaming and wailing grew worse like the howling cry of a lonely hurt wolf. Angelisa passed out of consciousness.

*****

Waking a few hours later, finding herself in the confines of the hospital emergency room, Angelisa held onto her husband's hand, releasing a flood of tears, and just cried, just cried, just cried.

After becoming calm and composed, she was discharged, her husband standing there, waiting to take her home.

Several days later, having complete control of herself, more determined to find her baby, Incerto, Angelisa met with Nurse Quinn. She brought Dunkin's and muffins for them. In a most gentle, calming way and in a soothing voice, she shared the facts of what happened at the center, choosing her words carefully and trying not to alarm Angelisa.

She shared with her that the babies, Prince and Princess, were not believed to be kidnapped but placed in the care of two rather affluent families who wanted a baby at any cost. She dared not say at this point, that it was speculated that the two infants were *sold through the Baby Black Market.*

Nurse Quinn sat with Angelisa for hours, holding her and soothing her. Nurse Quinn left after sharing with Angelisa what their next steps would be. They would have to meet with the police, the detectives assigned to the case, and the administrators of DCF, as well as the FBI, and definitely the Children's Advocacy Group and Human Rights Watch.

However, Angelisa was determined to go to the center to meet with Mila and Verinka. But she must approach the matter sensibly, calmly, with a sympathetic caring attitude for all the babies at the center. She also knew that she must let them understand the reasoning behind her emotional reaction to the news, her love for and caring for the babies, for all the babies.

And so that evening, with a howling wind and a cold mist blanketing the night, Angelisa plotted her carefully designed visit to the center. With heavy eyelids and streaming tears, Angelisa finally fell to sleep.

*****

The following day in the cold gray light of dawn, she put on her scarf, gloves, and heavy parka for protection from the cold. But what protection did these babies have? Who was protecting Prince and Princess, her Incerto?

Driving to the center, she became more determined and more horrified at the prospect that she may not find Incerto, may never see him, never hold him again, or snuggle with him by the warmth of the fireside. "No!" she screamed aloud, "I will find out the truth, and I WILL FIND HIM!"

As she approached the doorway, one of the younger assistants opened the door for her, placing her arm around her shoulders with a comforting gesture. Angelisa looked up and smiled a sad, aching, lonely smile.

Just then Mila came scurrying in from the visitor's room. She greeted her, hurrying her into the adjacent room.

"Angelisa, I'm so worry. You're no blame. A terrible thing happen. All worry and afraid for the babies. We tell we know. Da?"

Angelisa turned to her and asked for Verinka, the director.

"She must be out of her mind by now with two babies gone? They are her responsibility to keep them safe. What happened? Please tell me!"

Mila became deafeningly silent.

"Mila, where is Verinka, is she okay? Let me speak to her, help her as best I can," she said, feigning compassion and concern.

Still no answer.

"MILA, ANSWER ME! WHERE IS VERINKA?"

"She not here. She gone," stammered Mila.

"Gone?"

"I don't understand. Tell me where she is! Why she isn't here! What's going on?"

Angelisa raced up the flight of stairs to Verinka's office, frenetically searching through her desk, her drawers, and files. Nothing.

Mila slowly and fearfully followed Angelisa.

"You see, I tell truth," she whispered.

"This doesn't make any sense!" screamed Angelisa. Unless… "Oh no, no, no! They're gone, aren't they, Mila? Gone…sold…aren't they? How many more did you and Verinka sell? You are not in Russia; do you hear me? We do not sell babies, human life…how much did you get paid? How many families paid for all those precious lives they had no right to? How many innocents whose life, whose identity, whose very being you stole? Mila, tell me I'm wrong, that I'm out of my head. TELL ME!"

Mila began to tremble and shake, crawling into a corner and sobbing.

"What else were you people selling on the Baby Black Market? Tell me! Maybe diapers, bottles, blankets, and formula? Stealing from these poor 'throwaways' as you put it. You will pay for this!"

And with that, Angelisa stormed out of the center, jumped into her car, and sped off.

Arriving at the police station, still shivering, and trembling uncontrollably, she begins to tell her story.

Immediately DCF, the Children's Advocacy Group, and the FBI were alerted. The wheels were set in motion. *Now what is next?* she thought. Turning to her husband and sons, she fell into their arms.

"Come on, Mom. Let's go home."

*****

That evening as Angelisa lay in bed, so many thoughts swirling in her head, she becomes even more determined to find Incerto. She will go back to the Parkway Center, find names, contacts, anything that may provide a clue however meaningful or not. She will threaten Mila to tell the true about the scheme. But how? Threatening her with the fact that she is an illegal, that she was aware of the scheme, that she will be deported back to her country, Russia, or jailed here in America. *But how do I prove it? How!*

And so, she contacts a private investigation firm, accesses social media, radio and television outlets for help at any cost, to help her find her precious Incerto.

The relentless grip of winter, cold and lonely with its frozen earth and bare trees take hold clinging to a heart pierced with grief and torment.

Years passed, torturous years, but Angelisa held onto the one hope that one day she will find Incerto. But did that day ever come...

The cool crisp days of fall, the crush of fallen leaves underfoot bring back a harvest of memories. Autumn shows us how beautiful it is to *let things go.*

*****

The doorbell rang. A young man answered.

"May I help you?"

The young stranger, somewhat younger than the man, asked if this is the home of Angelisa Altomonte.

Hesitant, stunned, the young man replied, "Yes. May I help you in any way?"

"I'd like to speak with her, if that's okay with you."

A pause, a deep swallow. "May I ask what this is all about?"

Hesitant, clearing his throat, the young stranger replied, "Well, actually I would like to speak directly to Mrs. Altomonte."

The young man, too, cleared his throat. "My mother passed away last week." Pausing, he continued, "Is there something I can help you with?"

"Yes, there is something I wanted to share with her."

With head lowered, eyes fixed on the carpeted floor, the young stranger reaches into his pocket and hands a shiny metal box to Angelisa's son, John.

"Where did you get this? Was there something inside it? Tell me, please."

"It is a journey. A long one. Do you have time?"

"Time? Time? I've had twenty years of time to think about, live with anguish over the *time* the child disappeared!"

"To begin with, I am a student of Criminal Justice at my local university. Each one of the students is randomly assigned to an unsolved case. My assignment was that of an infant about three months old. Both the boy and the girl infants, Prince and Princess as named by your mother, went missing from a pre-foster care facility in Revere, the Parkway Infants and Toddler Center.

"I have studied all the facts associated with the case but was intrigued as to the reason this one volunteer was so passionately involved. Upon further investigation, I learned that the child, who was in fact sold on the Baby Black Market, was a foundling. However, she never regarded him as such. In her eyes, he was hers. Given to her to protect and love through God. Unfortunately, with all her attempts to find him, she was unsuccessful, which brings me to this, your mother's home. I began to come to know her—her love, hope, and unending determination to find the baby."

"Well, you have come to the right home. To a home that for years searched, followed every lead, every clue, hoping, praying to find this child. As my mother would say, 'this *gift from heaven*.' We did know that Incerto, my brother, that's the child's name, and the trafficking of the Russian Baby Black Market organization were involved. We searched and prayed for years not only hoping to find him but also praying that his life is good. You understand, don't you? My mom would often pray and say to these babies, 'You were born to dance to the beat of your own heart.' She held onto that dream."

"Thank you for that information. It helps me to put the pieces together and perhaps solve the disappearance of...did you say Incerto?"

"That's right. His two names became a combination of my name and my younger brother Carl...a Spanish version, and my mom's great-grandfather... Incerto GianCarlo. My mother believed he should hold onto, love, and keep his birth culture, therefore the name Incerto."

"Thank you for your intimate sharing," said the stranger. "I must share with you that this St. Ann's medal was seen in one of the photographs that your mother secretly took while at the center."

"Yes, she was hoping to capture the dire conditions under which the babies lived to show as proof to the authorities. It was Incerto's medal."

"It appears she was successful. She was instrumental in having the facility closed. Unfortunately, the director and her assistant were never brought to justice."

"You certainly did some great investigating. You're right, that was the medal of St. Ann. She saw to it that Incerto always had it on him or near him, no matter what."

Slowly, with hands trembling, the stranger opened the shiny metal box and carefully, reverently removed a medal, the medal of St. Ann.

Tears welling up in John's eyes, he turned his head to look away, to hide his tears.

"How, may I ask, that you happen to have it in your possession? Did you find it in the police evidence locker?

"It's a complicated story. I don't know if you have the time."

John staring intently at the stranger, waits for the moment of truth. "Please continue. I must know the truth."

"I must tell you that the facts of this child's disappearance are extremely difficult for me to share. I have not told anyone up to this point in time. As I told you, I had been assigned this cold case in my Criminal Justice Program at the Northeastern University, if you would like to verify my facts. By chance or by providence, who knows, I was assigned the case of one of the two babies *abducted*, that is the term used since the authorities did not really know if they were abducted, sold on the Black Market, or perhaps even dead by the time the investigation was completed.

"As I searched through a myriad of papers, eyewitness accounts, photographs, anonymous tips, and many photographs, one caught my eye, that of Blessed Mary's mother, St. Ann.

"I looked at it again while increasing the size visually, studying the details… And then I realized that I had seen it somewhere… I recognized it!

"That evening, as I returned home from class, the picture of that medal began to haunt me, just wouldn't leave my mind. Where did I see it? I know I saw it someplace before I saw it in the photograph. Was it one and the same? But how? Where did I see it? Am I imagining I saw it?

"And then, haunting memories came flashing in and out of my mind. My mother's jewelry box! I remember. I was quite the inquisitive child at that time to the point of being a nuisance. Always asking questions, always searching in the house, the garage, the storage rooms, making up mystery stories, driving my parents crazy.

"As I grew older, there was always this nagging question in my soul. I was told that I had been adopted as a baby, but there were no further details discussed. And eventually no further nagging questions from me. There was just *silence*. I decided that it was better to leave unanswered questions alone until able to find the truth, to understand the truth, and to accept the truth.

"So you see, John, the truth is not that simple to come by.

"Several evenings ago, I decided to confront the issue head on. Why? Why did I always have this gnawing feeling that there was more to my story? My adoptive family was quite affluent, never did I have a want, but never did I get those spontaneous, hugs, tickles, laughs you see children enjoying in the movies or even in cartoons. I just reasoned that it was their way, a part of their culture, their family upbringing to avoid any outward display of affection. Why? I just dismissed it, put it out of my mind. Told myself not to obsess over it.

"But when I began to investigate the disappearances, I found there were more incidents of children disappearing from Parkway Center that neither your mother nor the public knew. Your mother's unrelenting pursuit of the truth became so public that all countries became aware and responsible for the safety and well-being of all children, of all God's little children. Only then did I realize the pain your mother endured and lived with all those years.

"As I began to research further online, there it was, the Medal of St. Ann. Forgive me for rambling on, John. I must share how I feel, what I know."

"Please go on… I, too, must know. I, too, feel your pain."

"That evening when I returned home, with that burden in my soul, I went directly to the master bedroom. Trembling within my entire being, I took out my mother's jewelry box, opened it, and there in plain view was the medal. Oh no, my heart cried, my soul cried. I stood there in disbelief, holding in my hand the 'treasure' I hunted for, but this time did not want to find.

"As I lay in bed that fall evening, wind howling through the trees, I think that as seasons change, so, too, will the seasons of my life."

*****

That following morning as we sat at the breakfast table, anxiety, fear enveloped my entire being. Do I speak now...do I share what I fear that which I always felt in my heart, my mind, my soul?

"Mom, Dad, remember when I was a little boy, all the make-believe hunts in the woods, in the jungles, and even to outer space? Well"—with a slight crack in his voice, a tremble—"last night, I went on another hunt, this time a real hunt, a search that I have been longing to do for so long, but was afraid, a search to find *me*."

Slowly, quietly, and gently he brought from his pocket the medal of St. Ann. He placed it with great care before his parents. Gasps of shock came from both parents followed by silence, a deadening, piercing silence.

"Would you care to explain...would you care to give back to me, me?"

Again silence. Then his father began.

"We never really went into detail because the circumstances were less *important* than actually having you as our son, *our* child."

"You must understand. We did not deliberately hide anything. All you had to do was to come and ask us. We would have answered all your questions, doubts, and fears. We had you, and that was all that mattered. Why, why after all this time you demand to know the details of your birth. You are ours, only ours."

"Paid and bought for all in a neat little package with a pretty blue medal to go with it."

"It wasn't like that. We were hurting and wanted a child oh so badly, and yes, quickly. When we were told of the Parkway Center, it sounded honest enough."

"How much did honesty cost?"

"For years, I have been sought after by a kind, loving woman to whom I had been given by my birth mother through love, not realizing the unforeseen pain it brought to the woman who was to be my appointed mother, my anointed mother by the angels above her. That woman was working at the center the night, I, along with another child, mysteriously disappeared, never to be found. You see this woman, let's call her Angelisa, quite the ethnic name, huh, searched her entire life looking for this baby...*me*.

"She died never knowing if I were still alive, who I was, would I ever find her... So let me finish the rest of my 'adventure.'

"Yesterday, I found her, more precisely I found her son, my God-given brother with whom I shared my pain, my hurt, my longing to find this *mother*."

"My intention was to leave the medal with him. But just as I was leaving, he placed it in my hand. Hold onto this medal. It is yours to pin to your firstborn. Our mother would like that."

"Then, just as I was leaving, he called out, 'By the way...I never did get your name.'"

"Turning slowly, tears in my eyes but joy in my heart, I shouted, 'I'M THE BOY CALLED...INCERTO.'"

*****

It was October again…a glorious October, all red and gold with mellow mornings filled with delicate mists and dews so heavy that everything glistened like a cloth of silver, when you can feel the breath of fall morning and evening…no days so calm, so tenderly solemn, and with such reverence in the air.

"John, Carl. Hey, guys, would you come down to the family room, please?" Dad called out.

With heavy thunderous footsteps, both sons sauntered into the family room, sitting with a plop and a bounce on the sofa.

"What's up, Dad?" Carl queried, not looking directly at him, not seeing the anxiety and the uneasiness engulfing his pale crease-ridden aged face.

"Are you okay, Dad? Something is troubling you, right? Just tell us. It's okay."

"Thanks, sons. You see here on the table are two envelopes, the content of which will surely have an impact on your life moving forward," he said, clearing his throat and breathing deeply.

"One is a letter from someone Mom worked with at the Parent and Child Center in Everett, the other from Mom herself. You see, the day Mom received the letter from her colleague and read the contents, she decided after giving it much thought, she decided some days later to write this note to you." Hands visibly shaking, voice quivering, Dad began to read, voice trembling.

"My dear sons, I asked your Dad not to share any of what you are about to learn until one month after my passing. The reason being that I did not feel it fair for you to feel an obligation to carry on the search I had for those long tedious years that were filled with so much disappointment, sorrow, and yes, angst. You had to embrace life, your life, and not be encumbered with the responsibility to carry on what was to be my mission in this, my life. Take comfort in my belief that *in every person's lifetime, some heartache may occur, but in quiet solitude, God helps us endure.* And so, I did. And did it with the *love I give to you.*"

With hands trembling, softly, quietly, the letter was folded and while putting it in the envelope, Dad brought it to his lips and gently placed a kiss on it.

Dad then picked up the other letter and carefully removed it from its yellowed, frayed envelope. He handed it to John to read to them its contents.

October 10, 1990

My Dear Miss Angelisa,

We here at the Family and Child Center are so sorry for what we know you are now going through. We share your pain, sorrow, and despair. You are in our prayers, even your little ones join in.

But your pain and sorrow are shared with the deepest grief, sorrow, and pain within a heart pierced with grief...the heart of Baby Incerto's birth mother, Maria DeLa Cruz.

A veil of deafening silence engulfed the room. Neither John, Carl, nor Dad spoke. Eyes wide, focused, glistening with shock and bewilderment.

John gulped and began to swallow, taking deep controlled breaths. He managed to squeak out the rest of the message.

> Miss Angelisa, a parent here at the center knew about Maria and her leaving the infant child with you. But being sworn to secrecy for fear of having the authorities or whomever find out her circumstances, she feared being arrested or worse. Which brings me to the note Maria herself was able to get to you.
>
> Miss Angelisa, oh my, Miss Angelisa, can there be any greater pain in life than to lose a child, no, to have a child ripped from your inner being, from your heart, from your soul? No!
>
> Please believe that you bear no responsibility. Do you not share the anguish, the disbelief as I do? Did we not hold our precious baby as an extension of us both? Do we not cry out to God to comfort us, to console us, to love us even more… Do we not cry out to God to keep our precious boy safe, secure and in the protection of the Holy Spirit?
>
> I love you, Miss Angelisa.

My heart cries, my soul weeps.

There was a silent hush in the room: no movement, no breath, no life. Moments later, John spoke up, "How did Mom carry this pain within her without saying a word, without sharing this burden? Now I understand her going off to her room and in her privacy and pain read and reread the letters. Well, I know what I...*no*, what *we* must do. We are going to find Incerto and put together the missing part of him, his life, his being."

Turning away, with tears welling up, shielding his face, Dad shuffled slowly toward the rocker and in an in almost suspended motion collapsed into it.

"Wait, Dad," calls Carl as he reaches out to help cushion his father as he sits. "I'll get the shawl to warm you."

Kneeling at the blanket chest, Carl began to ruffle through the many colorful, hand-knitted, crocheted, stitched coverings, settling upon a soft, textured shawl, a blend of azure, lilac, and pink yarns creating a tapestry of the sky. Carl gently placed the shawl around Dad's shoulders when suddenly, across the room they heard a long low-moaning cry like the piercing sound of a hurt animal in the wild.

Carl jerked around to see his brother John's shoulders falling, chest caving in, body swaying slightly. Carl dashed over to catch his brother from falling while he lifted him to the sofa.

"What is it, John? What happened? Are you alright? Tell me screeches!" Carl shouted.

As John began to regain composure, with chin resting on chest, he slowly raised his head, eyes fixed upon the shawl, gently touching it and cried out, "It's Baby Incerto's shawl… Why now, why at this time… It feels like past memories are becoming one within us. We must find Incerto, we must complete our mother's journey, her quest, bring lasting peace to her."

And with that said, the loves of Angelisa Altomonte sat quietly in solemn silence.

*****

A gentle hush cloaked the ground that following morning. The empty skies were bare, silent. Winter smothered the land.

While sitting at the breakfast table that morning, John, and Carl were devising a plan to locate, search for, find once again the boy called Incerto. But how? Where do they start? They do not know his rightful name that he received from his adoptive parents.

Then John remembered something from his meet with Incerto a month back. Incerto was attending college, studying criminal justice. But where, what school?

With so many colleges and universities in the Boston area, he surely must be enrolled at one of them. Then both brothers began the alphabet memory game. Each would name a letter of the alphabet and say as many schools that begin with that letter (e.g., A—Amherst, B—Boston College, Boston University, etc.) until the name of a familiar school, "rings a bell." Alternating a letter each, John suddenly stopped.

"I've got it! Northeastern University in Boston on Huntington Avenue."

Carl then went to the computer, googled the university, and a myriad of information popped up.

"We'll go tomorrow. Meet with the department head and share with him our search."

"I think, dear brother, we should first call to make an appointment. Time is of the essence. Let's get this done for Mom and Dad's sake, our sake, and especially, Incerto's."

*****

Stepping out into the snow, their boots crunched, their teeth chattered, their body shivered. Yes, winter was stifling the world with its icy breath.

Nothing would deter these brothers from finding their baby brother once again.

While inside the university, swallowing up the warmth that engulfed them, John and Carl stopped at the fourth floor and followed the sign to the School of Criminology and Criminal Justice.

John tapped quietly on the glass office door window.

"Come in, Mr. Altomonte," a quiet, demure voice called out.

Entering the office, John was greeted by Ms. Callahan, a pert, petite, personable young lady, certainly not the administrator he had envisioned.

"So I understand, Mr. Altomonte, that you came here hoping to find the identity of one of our former students. Criminology major?"

"That's correct. This matter is of a personal nature, so to speak."

"In what way, if I may ask? To share personal information about any student is highly unusual and seldom done by the university. There has to be an overwhelmingly urgent, imminently necessary reason for this request. So please do inform me of the nature of your request."

Outside the office, Carl sat comfortably in the leather-padded armchair, flipping through the school brochure, while inside the office, John's stomach was doing flip-flops.

"What I am about to share is of the most personal nature touching the heart and soul of any being. You see, Ms. Callahan, this young stranger became a foundling shortly after his birth. He was placed in my mother's care, never knowing the identity of his birth mother.

"One day, by the hand of providence, this young stranger shows up at my mother's home asking for her. I told him the heart-breaking news that my mom had passed that week. Visibly upset, the young man asked if he may come into the house. I ushered him in as he looked around the room, taking in every nook and cranny, asking questions of genuine curiosity and interest.

"Motioning him to sit on the sofa, he appeared to become more relaxed and comfortable. And then, clearing his throat, he asked if my mother were the lady who searched for an abducted baby many years ago.

"Naturally, I was stunned, taken aback to be asked about something that happened so long ago. I asked him why he wanted to know. This young stranger then told me the story of his being a student at this university and being randomly assigned as part of the course, the cold case of a baby abducted some twenty years ago. Through his research, he became very taken by the story. He wanted so desperately to follow all the clues and to put my mother's mind at rest. It appears he was profoundly affected by this case, and so he decided to seek out my mother if just to see her, to tell her how he admired her compassion and concern for all foundling babies. And yet he himself could not deny the passion, the frustration, and sadness deep within for this baby and others *stolen, ripped from their mother's heart.*

"Closing his eyes and taking in a deep breath, he gently took from his pocket a small satin sack and handed it to me. He wanted my mother, now me, to keep this as a remembrance of her perseverance, determination, yes, hope in trying to find this baby who carried the medal of St. Ann. With a quivering smile, he rushed out the door."

Using a quiet voice, Ms. Callahan said, "A very moving story. However, you still have not told me your reason for trying to locate this young stranger."

"It will all become clear now. You see, my mother, many years ago received a letter from one of her colleagues. Her colleague shared with her the name of the foundling's birth mother. She also described the shawl the baby was wrapped in, pinned with the medal of St. Ann. Coincidence, I think not. There is something neither of us can explain. This strong, this visceral feeling he felt inside him, seeking to reconnect with the young stranger to perhaps give him and myself answers to so many questions unspoken. I felt my only hope was to find his name here since awhile back he was a student here. So, will you please help me, help him, Ms. Callahan?"

Using a quiet voice and with a slight smile, Ms. Callahan walked slowly to the computer and brought up his name, Justin Marchand.

*****

The empty skies were silent. Their crunching was a heaviness to the air—if you stood still and tried to breathe as quietly as possible, then the sound of silence could be deafening.

John and Carl, their bodies shivering, fingertips tingling, trudged slowly to their car, snow crunching beneath their boots.

Opening the door to their home, they were greeted by the joyous flames of the fire leaping, crackling, and hissing into life, creating an overall flutter in the stomach, an overall relaxation of the body.

The brothers then shared the good news with their dad. Now a plan had to be put in place. Justin Marchand, their foundling baby brother, must be *found* again. Each had a part of the plan to fulfill: Carl—google his name, address, and iPhone or cell number. John—contact the colleague who wrote to his mother and get the address and phone number of his birth mother, Maria DeLa Cruz.

During that day, both brothers were feverishly working, calling, writing, texting to compile as much information as possible.

Fortunately, John was able to contact Natalia Hernandez, who was still at the Mother-Child Center in Everett. He obtained the birth mother's address and the name of a close relative. He also got Ms. Hernandez's email address.

Later, John would recall how emotional Ms. Hernandez became to hear his voice and to realize the possibility of finding the boy called Incerto.

Carl worked on contacting the Marchands, which he did, and left a voice message for Justin to call the Altomonte brothers. Very important!

With the wheels in motion, the brothers had to bide their time and wait.

Later that evening, Incerto called to say that he would meet with them.

While driving to meet up with the brothers, Incerto looked around at the white snow blanketing the trees, the ground, the homes. All was so quiet, yet his mind was in a frenzy. What could be so imperative? His mind vacillated between panic and peace.

Taking deep, controlled breaths, Incerto rang the doorbell. Being greeted heartily, upon entering, he could hear the fire crackling, conversation cackling in the television, and the sweet smell of hot chocolate warmed in mugs set on a tray.

After introductions were made, John invited Incerto to the floor below and into the "man cave."

"Be seated, Justin." John motioned. "I have come across something important that I need to share with you. Understand, Justin, this information has to be borne out."

"I understand, John. But when I'm in this home, Miss Angelisa's home, I prefer you call me Incerto."

"Now I'm confused. Your given name *is* Justin Marchand, is it not?" queried John.

"It is, but I feel no longer comfortable with it. I feel I'm walking around in someone else's skin," whined Incerto, tense and upright, avoiding eye contact.

"Incerto is not your skin!" shouted John. "How much of a self-pitying ingrate have you become? Think of what your life, your existence has been up until now. How horribly were you treated by these parents, yes, adoptive parents who provided you with a peaceful, calm, and comfortable home, with food, clothing, all your wants satisfied. Think about it!

"Contemplate in the silence of your room tonight what your life would have been like, perhaps just as those 'abandoned' babies' lives could have been if not adopted or placed in foster care, to say the least. Tell me, share with me the horrible existence you have had with these two unselfish people who, yes, did buy you. Was it morally right? No. Was their heart in the right place? Yes. Did they not want you at any cost? Yes. Do not be so judgmental!

"What they did was motivated from the heart. Tell me, when you were a young child and had a bad dream or saw monsters on your bedroom wall, who did you call? Did your mother not soothe and comfort you? Do you just toss aside all the loving and caring they gave? Yes, your world, at this point in your life, has been turned upside down. Step out of your *skin*, and try walking around in theirs."

Rubbing the back of his neck, John muttered that was all he had to say right now. He walked Incerto to the door and said good night.

*****

That evening, Incerto laid in bed, mulled over and over in his mind the scorching words John rained upon him, words that moved him to tears, but more importantly caused him to look inside himself, to be self-reflective. Indeed, there was a void internally that only he could fill with accepting who he was at that moment: Justin Marchand, adopted by caring, devoted parents who deserve respect instead of scorn; gratitude instead of resentment; admiration instead of bitterness.

For days, the city was snowbound, arctic white. The empty skies were silent. Incerto felt like winter had stifled all life, his life. He contemplated John's words. *Go home, Incerto. You need to be alone to sort out your feelings. Think, pray, run, shout, let it all out. Exhaust yourself physically, emotionally, then contemplate.*

Remember, the Holy Spirit will guide you. And so, it did. It was time to listen to my heart, my soul, my entire being.

Later that evening, Incerto quietly descended the stairs leading to the family room where his parents sat wrapped in each other's arms, before the crackling hissing fire, gazing intensely as the embers escaped.

Just then, Incerto stood in front of them, wet dull eyes, trembling chin, sagging shoulders, he fell to his knees as a supplicant, placed his head on his mother's lap, his hand on his father's knee, and sobbed. Words were not necessary; *love* filled the room.

Callous winter released its viselike grip and breathed life into the land, into the skies, into Incerto.

*****

That afternoon Incerto found himself at the home of the Altomonte family, praying that John be home. A ring of the buzzer, and John appeared before Incerto, stunned but happy. With a smile and arm around his shoulder, John escorted Incerto once again to the "man cave."

"I am glad you decided to come back, Incerto. What I have to share with you came as unexpectedly to my family, in fact, shockingly unexpected as I am sure it will to you. You see, Incerto, my mom left a letter for me and my brother, Carl, to open and read one month after her passing."

A slight quiver could be heard in John's voice, a slight shaking of the letter in his hand, a slight glance aside. Choosing his words with care, placing a hand on his shoulder, John told Incerto the name and country of his birth mother.

"Your birth mother's name is Maria DeLa Cruz, and she lives in the Dominican Republic."

Incerto slowly got up from the sofa and walked to the back of the room, needing space, needing time to process this information. He became speechless, taking shaky breaths, shielding his face, tears welling up as he digested the shocking information. Then glancing around without really seeing anything, Incerto stammered, "Is this possible, is this true. I don't understand. How, after all these years?"

"It is true, Incerto. My mom's colleague, Natalia Hernandez, brought all this information to her in a letter written twenty years ago. I know it's hard to handle right now, but my mom often shared with me and my brother, Carl, her belief that *in every person's lifetime, some heartache may occur, but in quiet solitude, God helps us endure.*"

*****

Within the first hour of sunrise, the flint grey sky of the evening had turned into a rainbow of yellow, pink, and orange. I marveled at the might of nature. The snow around me flashed and glittered like angel-fire. My soul rejoiced.

That day I found myself at John's door. This time I took deep, calming breaths. Joyful tears released themselves from my eyes.

John came to the door, opened it, ushered me in staring deeply into my eyes, pausing, then said, "Are you ready to take the first step toward the rest of your life?"

Plans were made, tickets bought, luggage packed, a new journey lay ahead. Life lay ahead. A willingness to believe everything will be all right lay ahead.

*****

The following morning, I boarded the plane for the Dominican Republic. Hours later, what seemed like an endless horizon, it landed at Las Americas International Airport.

Arrangements had been made with Eliana, my birth mother's niece, to meet me when I landed. I dialed her number with my mobile phone and in my best, "broken" Spanish told her I had arrived. In English, she directed me to her blue Hyundai parked in the pickup area.

As I walked with my travel bag clutched closely to my chest, I spotted the car with a young twentyish looking girl standing next to it.

"Welcome to Barahona," my cousin said while opening the door on the left-hand side of the car. She entered on the right side, which is the driver's side in the DR (Dominican Republic). We exchanged all the polite amenities while we drove on the Enriguello Highway, which she pointed out was considered one of the busiest streets in the province of Barahona. She continued to point out that on my left was the Caribbean Sea, which sparkles turquoise while the mountains of Barahona tower on my right. Along the way, wooden houses with colorful roofs pop up against the wilderness. Eliana then continued in an attempt to relieve the deadening silence; the Barahone Province is often referred to as Caribbean's Brides. That is because the best wedding venues are located throughout the area.

Then I looked at Eliana and said, "Tell me about Maria DeLa Cruz, my birth mother."

As her smile began to grow, Eliana turned toward Incerto and described her as the sweetest, kindest, loving human being to walk this earth. "Soon after *mi tia* returned to Barahona, she went to live with her sister, my mother, and me. Excuse me, sometimes I slip into my native language. I meant, my aunt."

In a lighter tone, I smiled and answered, "No problemo." At that, both broke out into soft laughter.

Eliana continued, "I must tell you that the horrific news of your being abducted darkened her entire world both literally and figuratively."

My voice quaking, choked with tears I shouted tell me something, anything, "Is it that my mother cannot see… that she is blind?"

Eliana looked away.

Adrenaline rushing through my body, dry throat from rushed breathing, pounding in my ears, I screamed a voiceless scream. Covering my mouth, I slumped back into the seat.

Eliana reached over and ever so lightly tapped my shoulder.

"It's called hysterical blindness, a functional or unexplained condition resulting from emotional trauma. The news of your abduction some twenty years ago was so overwhelmingly crushing that your birth mother became visually paralyzed. She has been that way ever since. We have taken her to several doctors including eye doctor, psychiatrist, and play therapist. We also had her work as an aid in a baby shelter to hold, rock, and sing to these children. All these attempts to help her did not work.

"However, being a strong and religious person, she has handled the situation with stoicism, with a sense of calm, with the belief that everything will work out, will be all right. And she is right. You, Incerto, will make everything all right again."

As they approached Uladislao Guerrero, Casa 10, Eliana turned off the engine to give Incerto a bit more time to regain his composure. Incerto, mind racing, came to grips with what had happened. A sense of calm enshrouded his entire being. Taking strong breaths, looking directly at Eliana, and smiling, he said, "I am ready." Eliana reached over to hold his hand tenderly. They both walked from the car, arm in arm, and rang the doorbell.

Eliana's youngest sister, Sonia, opened the door to let them in, all the while staring at Incerto.

Eliana offered Incerto a seat in the living room, but he nodded, preferring to stand, to wait, and to behold his birth mother as she approached him for the first time.

Heart pounding, breathless, and tingling all over, Incerto closed his eyes, hand covering his mouth, feeling the need to touch his birth mother as she walked toward him.

Eliana guided her aunt Maria to the sofa, smoothing out the pillows as she tipped her head back and closed her eyes. Eliana, holding Maria's warm, slender hands, whispered to her that Incerto was here in the room with them.

Maria, placing her hand over her heart, eyes that are soft, filled with an inner glow, motioned Incerto to sit near to her on the sofa.

Pulling in deep breaths and holding them until all tensions left the body, believing that everything in one's life has aligned, Incerto slowly and quietly sat down on the sofa. Maria slowly angled her body toward Incerto and softly, gently began to trace the contours of his face. With soft warm fingertips, she traced his eyes, outlined his nose, fingered the shape of his lips, touching, smoothing, caressing his entire face with loving hands, paused, and began to cry.

Incerto took her hands in his, slowly lifting them to his face and placed a soft, warm, euphoric kiss upon them. He, too, shed tears of love. Then slowly, Incerto reached for his backpack, opened it, and removed two items: a tissue-wrapped object and a smaller silver-wrapped package. He placed on his mother's lap the larger, tissue-wrapped object. With care and a look of puzzlement, Maria unwrapped the package. She stopped, breathed in the fabric, and let out a moan, holding tightly to her bosom the shawl of azure, lilac, and pink yarns, reflecting the sky's tapestry, her *baby boy's* shawl, *Incerto's* shawl. Then, almost unnoticed, Incerto placed in her lap the silver-wrapped box. With trembling fingers, Maria unwrapped the tiny box and fingered around inside when suddenly she stopped, startled, frozen throughout her being. Slowly, gently, trembling, she took from the silver-wrapped box a tiny object, brought it to her lips, kissed it while signing herself, crossing herself, sobbing while tears trickled down. She shouted out with elation, "Mi bebe ha vuelto a casa!"

"I am here, Mother," whispered Incerto, voice cracking with emotion, clasping his mother so tenderly to his breast. "I will always be here for you."

After the long, dark winter months passed, spring is literally a breath of fresh air. It is the time of year when everything in nature is changing and promising new life and new hope as it would for Maria DeLa Cruz and her son Incerto.

ABOUT THE AUTHOR

This is author Christine Marano's first attempt at writing a novel. She is no stranger to this writing genre. She received first prize for a short story she wrote while in high school in Boston. Her prize was a copy of *Arabian Nights*, which she treasures. She is an avid reader. She refuses to use social media in place of personalized greetings. Christine has been a special education teacher for the past forty years. She is also an education surrogate for the juvenile court system in Massachusetts. This background contributes to the theme of this novel. She lives just outside of Boston with her husband, Pasquale, and two cats, Pino and Grigio, and babysits her gal, Mumma, her son's loving, loyal pit bull. Christine has two adult sons, Peter, and Vincent.

CPSIA information can be obtained
at www.ICGtesting.com
Printed in the USA
LVHW030536231121
704215LV00009B/308

9 781638 853657